SO-AET-769

The Old Wagoner

Idella Bodie

SANDLAPPER PUBLISHING CO., INC.
ORANGEBURG, SOUTH CAROLINA 29115

Copyright © 2002 Idella Bodie

All rights reserved.

FIRST EDITION

Published by Sandlapper Publishing Co., Inc.
Orangeburg, South Carolina 29115

MANUFACTURED IN THE UNITED STATES OF AMERICA

Cover illustration courtesy of South Caroliniana Library

Library of Congress Cataloging-in-Publication Data

Bodie, Idella.
    The old wagoner / Idella Bodie.— 1st ed.
      p. cm. — (Heroes and heroines of the American Revolution)
    Summary: Describes the childhood, military service, and accomplishments
of Daniel Morgan, especially as they relate to the southern campaigns of the
American Revolution.
    Includes bibliographical references.
    ISBN 0-87844-165-4
    1. Morgan, Daniel, 1736-1802—Juvenile literature. 2. Generals—United
States—Biography—Juvenile literature. 3. United States. Continental Army—
Biography. 4. United States—History—Revolution, 1775-1783—Cam-
paigns—Juvenile literature. 5. Southern States—History—Revolution, 1775-
1783—Campaigns—Juvenile literature. [1. Morgan, Daniel, 1736-1802. 2.
Generals. 3. United States. Continental Army. 4. United States—History—
Revolution, 1775-1783.] I. Title.

E207.M8 B63 2002
973.3'3'092—dc21
[B]

                                       2002030242

Acknowledgements

I am indebted to Don Higginbotham for his fine work, *Daniel Morgan: Revolutionary Rifleman.*

I wish to express my appreciation to the staff of Cowpens National Battlefield, Rangers Patricia Ruff and Scott Withrow, who read the manuscript and offered invaluable advice.

I'd also like to acknowledge my editor, Barbara Stone, without whose diligence and dedication this series would not be possible.

To the Young Reader

Daniel Morgan's story begins before the Revolutionary War when England still governed the colonies. Also at this time in history, France and England fought over unsettled land in America.

As a young man, Daniel drove a supply wagon with food, ammunition, and other provisions for the British army. Although he was not old, he earned the nickname of "The Old Wagoner." He even called himself that in talking to others.

Morgan's fame as a soldier came when he fought for the British in the French and Indian War. Native Americans, who had long occupied these lands, joined the British or the French. Each side made promises of treating the Indians right when the battle was over.

At the outbreak of the Revolutionary War, Morgan joined the Patriots and led a company of sharpshooting riflemen in a northern battle.

When the thickest fighting moved to the southern colonies, the upcountry of South Carolina was a frontier land with grassy plains and natural springs. It was here in the battle of Cowpens that Morgan went down in history as commander of one of the most important battles in the Revolutionary War.

Contents

1.
The Boy from Nowhere

At the age of seventeen, Daniel Morgan had a fight with his father. He left home with only the clothes he wore. From then on it appears that Daniel never looked back. As far as anyone knows, he never mentioned where he was born or who his parents were. Those who knew Daniel felt he had an unhappy childhood as he never talked about it. It is believed he was born about 1736 in Hunterdon

County, New Jersey, to poor Welsh immigrants and his father worked as a farm laborer.

Daniel headed south along the Great Wagon Road through Pennsylvania to North Carolina. He probably joined others who searched for a better life.

On the way south he stopped to work at odd jobs. Already six feet, two inches tall and weighing over two hundred pounds, he had no trouble finding farm work.

By spring he had a job on a farm in Frederick County, Virginia. He was a strong, hard worker and soon became foreman of the owner's sawmill. Daniel had barely gotten into his new job when a man from the nearby village of Winchester talked him into driving a wagon.

A restless, high-spirited youth, Daniel liked the idea of being a wagoner. That job would give him more freedom and more money. Besides, he liked the owner of the wagon company, John Ashby. John liked riding his horse, shooting his rifle, and drinking rum at a local tavern.

When Daniel wasn't hauling supplies like tar, nails, flour, salt, and rum to the frontier people, he went to the tavern too. He liked to joke and clown around with the other men. He played cards and drank rum.

By now he was a giant of a man with powerful arms and shoulders and rocklike fists. He liked to wrestle and he became the champion wrestler in the Shenandoah Valley.

One thing that got Daniel into trouble was his fiery temper. He did not like to be criticized. If anybody said something to him or about him he did not like, he usually ended up in a fight. When he wasn't in a brawl, he had good times with his friends.

He managed to save part of his salary and within a year he had enough money to start his own business. He bought a team of horses and a wagon and began hauling things for other people.

Daniel liked his career as an independent wagoner, but he never dreamed what he would one day haul in his wagon.

2.
The Old Wagoner

Before the Revolutionary War began, the French and British fought for North American land not yet claimed by other countries. This period of fighting became known as the French and Indian War because some Indians helped the British and others helped the French.

When the British decided to attack the French at Fort Duquesne, they assigned British general Edward Braddock to that unsettled country near the Great Lakes. He commanded his soldiers and a small group of Virginians under George Washington, who was then a young man. Braddock needed wagoners to carry his army's equipment. He came to the

Shenandoah Valley, where Daniel lived, looking for wagoners, sometimes called teamsters, who owned their teams of horses or mules.

Always ready for adventure and money, Morgan signed up. He loaded his wagon with army supplies and traveled over the rough wilderness roads. He handled his team of horses well.

British officers found the Valley wagoners a rowdy bunch.

They fought among themselves and with the red-coated soldiers. They gambled and drank. Finally, the officers decided they would no longer put up with such behavior. They warned that from this time on wagoners would follow the same rules as the fort soldiers. Anyone disobeying the rules would be lashed with a whip on his bare back.

One spring day Daniel angered a British lieutenant. The officer struck Daniel with the flat of his sword. With one blow of his huge fist, Daniel knocked the man out cold. He was sentenced to 500 lashes.

Daniel yanked off his hunting shirt and waited for the drummer to beat out the count of each whiplash across his broad shoulders. It is said that from the first beat Daniel counted along with the drummer. When the punishment ended, flesh hung from his bloody back.

"The drummer missed a count," he told over and over to friends and eager listeners. "But I did not see the need to tell him that he gave me only 499."

Once the pain and anger left him, Morgan said, "I would not take anything for the whipping. It gave me a story that will never grow old."

With the Indians' help, the French won the battle at Fort Duquesne. The defeated British army headed back to the colonies. This time Morgan carried wounded soldiers in his wagon.

It was during the French and Indian War that Daniel was given the nickname "The Old Wagoner." The name stuck throughout his life. He even spoke of himself that way.

3.
Family Man

Back in Frederick County, Virginia, Morgan learned that his friend, John Ashby, was now a captain with the Virginia rangers. The rangers patrolled the frontier protecting colonists from Indians who sided with the French. Ashby talked Morgan into joining them.

On one occasion when Morgan guided a militia of rangers, seven Indians sprang from ambush and opened fire. A musket ball tore into Morgan's neck, passed through his cheek, and knocked out his teeth on the left side. He managed to stay in his saddle until he returned to the fort.

When the frontier became safer, Morgan went back to his wagoning, carrying needed products to the frontier settlers. In between hauls, he played cards with other wagoners at a neighborhood store. He also visited a tavern at a settlement called Battletown. He and other frontiersmen enjoyed wrestling and racing on foot and on horseback. No one could beat Morgan. After he won at wrestling, he would slap his opponent on the back and say, "You came close!"

Then something happened to Morgan that changed his interests. In Winchester, Virginia, he met Abigail Curry, the daughter of a well-to-do farmer. Because he wanted Abigail to like him, he began to take an interest in his appearance. Sales records from an old store where he shopped show he bought new clothes, "a gentleman's hat," a watch, a comb, and cuff links for his shirt sleeves. He also bought a lady's handkerchief, silk cloth, and ribbons.

Instead of visiting with his friends after work, Morgan unhitched his team and changed from his fringed buckskin "Indian clothes" into his new ones to visit Abigail and take her gifts. He visited her often, always with gifts, until he finally won her heart.

The two were as different as any two people could be. Abigail was a lady. Besides having good manners, she was educated and religious. She liked Morgan, but she could not bear his sport of fist fighting.

When a powerful young fellow from the Blue Ridge Mountains beat Morgan in a fight, Abigail scolded him and begged him to change his ways.

Morgan promised that once he whipped the fellow to show him he could, he would give up fighting. The next day Morgan fought the man and won. True to his word, he never fought with his fists again.

Abigail was a good influence on Morgan. Soon they were married. The couple had two daughters, Nancy and Betsy. Abigail did not completely tame her husband, but she made a difference. With family responsibilities, Morgan turned his life in a different direction. He bought a home and land, where he became a tobacco farmer.

In time, Morgan gained the respect of important citizens in their community, including his minister. The attitudes of others showed him that a man's worth is measured by the way he acts and talks now, not on what he has done in the past.

4.
Call to Arms

At this time in history, America was a wilderness. Frontier life was hard. Morgan, like other frontiersmen, depended on his hunting rifle to provide meat for his family. These rugged, lean men, weathered by sun and wind, wore hunting shirts, leggings, and moccasins like the Indians. Their clothing, the color of dried leaves, blended with the woods. Also like the Indians, a tomahawk and a knife hung from each man's belt.

Morgan and other colonists had heard of the unrest of the colonies toward their mother country of England, particularly in the North. It did not come as a complete surprise when news reached them of the shot "heard round the world." The Revolutionary War had begun.

The Continental Congress asked Morgan to form companies of riflemen to aid in the cause of freedom. Although he did not want to leave his family and farm, he saddled his horse.

For weeks he rode over the countryside of Frederick County, Virginia, in search of hunters to join in the fight. When meeting them, he told

stories of the glory of defending one's country. Some of the men he met had fought with him against the Indians. Convincing the marksmen they were needed in the North, he rounded up even more volunteers than Congress requested.

"I have an old score to settle with the British," he explained.

For three weeks Morgan trained his men. To get them pepped up, he had contests to see who was the best shot. In their hunting clothes, which served as their uniforms, the men paraded by the Winchester courthouse, the church, and the tavern for everyone to see. The townspeople cheered them.

With training completed, the company of soldiers began its 600-mile march from Virginia to

Cambridge, Massachusetts. As the men marched, people of the towns and villages turned out to see them. Small boys and barking dogs ran along beside them. For the twenty-three days of the march, in all kinds of weather, colonists lined up along the roads to cheer them on.

Much to the enjoyment of the citizens, Morgan allowed the men to use enough ammunition to show off their marksmanship. Those who saw the display found it hard to believe.

5.
Taken Prisoner

George Washington, now commander in chief of the Patriot forces, was organizing an army to invade British-held Quebec by going through Maine. General Washington put Colonel Benedict Arnold in charge of capturing Quebec. Arnold felt the frontiersmen could withstand the hardships of the Maine wilderness better than soldiers from New England who had been clerks, farmers, and fishermen. Because of that, he asked Daniel Morgan to get his militia ready to march.

Drums rolled and fifes sounded as Morgan's riflemen headed toward the coast to board a fleet of small ships that would carry them to Maine.

Once on land, their march to Quebec became a nightmare. In bitterly cold weather and howling wind they trudged along where no roads existed. Fallen trees and bogs slowed them down. They sloshed through mud, sinking half-leg deep.

Waterfalls kept them from putting their boats on rivers. Carrying them wore away flesh from their shoulders. Rain put out the fires they built to dry their clothing. It also ruined much of their food. Soldiers held rifles and muskets under their coats to keep them dry. Many became ill, but they pushed on. When the food gave out, soldiers roasted saddle bags and ate a mixture of shaving soap and lip salve.

Finally, Benedict Arnold sent out a relief force to meet them. The troop brought oatmeal, flour, and cattle. Soldiers killed the cattle and cut the meat into pieces for cooking. Too starved to wait for the meat to be cooked, many of the soldiers ate it raw.

The nasty weather finally worked in favor of Morgan's men—a blizzard hid their arrival at

Quebec. But it also gave the British more time to get ready to fight.

Quebec sat on high cliffs above the St. Lawrence River. To their disappointment, Arnold's troops failed to take the town. It was said if Arnold had listened to Morgan, they might not have been defeated.

Morgan became so angry about the surrender he burst into tears. Even with a gun pointed at him, he refused to give up his sword to the British army. Finally, he handed it over to a priest in the crowd.

To make matters worse, he and others became prisoners of war. The British officers knew of Morgan's reputation. They admired him and treated him kindly. They even asked him to come over to their side, promising to make him a colonel.

Morgan answered, "I am not a scoundrel. My services are not for sale."

After eight months, Morgan was freed in exchange for a British officer. He and other freed prisoners returned by ship to the shore of New Jersey. Upon reaching Patriot soil, some men wept. Some laughed with glee, hugging fellow soldiers. Others whooped and hollered. Morgan is said to have fallen to the ground with his arms outspread and cried, "Oh, my country!"

6.
Helping Out in the North

When Morgan returned to his home, which he called Soldier's Rest, he found his wife and two daughters well. But they had worried about his safety.

Morgan's reputation as a leader spread. Congress commissioned him to the rank of colonel and gave him command of the 11th Virginia regiment. He left home once again, determined to make his regiment the finest in the army.

Although Morgan's temper exploded now and then and his powerful fists occasionally bruised soldiers who did not follow rules, riflemen knew him to be fair and just. He forbade public whippings. "It breaks a man's spirit," he said. Instead, he encouraged his men to seek him out if they had problems.

He also tried to promote good feelings between officers and enlisted men. Morgan became known for his ability to lead soldiers. They respected him and pushed themselves harder for him.

The tale is told that once he saw two of his riflemen sweating and straining as they tried to move a large rock from the road. Seeing an officer nearby, Morgan asked, "Why don't you lay hold and help these men?"

"Sir," the man replied, "I am an officer."

"I BEG YOUR PARDON," thundered Morgan. "I did not think of that."

Then he jumped from his horse and gave the soldiers a hand in rolling away the stone.

George Washington constantly asked for

Morgan's services. Morgan's riflemen were said to be the commander in chief's pride and joy. His sharpshooters fought in the battles at Saratoga.

7.
Praise for Morgan

In one attack, as Morgan galloped back and forth to hold his battle line, enemy fire shot his horse from under him. Henry Dearborn and his troop of musketmen rushed in to protect their commander from the thrust of British bayonets. Morgan was quick to credit his officer for saving his life and the lives of his riflemen.

After Saratoga, General Horatio Gates said, "Too much praise cannot be given to the corps commanded by Morgan."

George Washington gave Morgan his warmest thanks for helping out in the North. Once when Morgan was with Washington, he met a striking, young French officer, the

Marquis de Layfayette. This Frenchman, who volunteered to help Americans in their fight for freedom, took a keen interest in Morgan. The polished nobleman and the crude frontiersman became good friends.

Later, when Morgan had the task of patrolling an area to keep Tories from supplying provisions to the British, he gained respect of all the country people, even Tories, with his fairness.

8.
Morgan Pulls Out

When Congress failed to give Morgan an assignment he wanted and a promotion, he suffered deep disappointment. He felt he had given himself to his country, even sacrificing his health. At the age of forty-four, he ached with rheumatism because of his hard army life. Sometimes the sciatic nerve in his hip hurt so much he could hardly sit in the saddle.

He had fought in more battles than any other Patriot colonel and been honored for his two battles at Saratoga. George Washington tried to talk Congress into promoting Morgan, but the men in power refused. Virginia already had enough generals they said.

Although Morgan rarely received pay, he considered the army his job. Before the war, he worked as a wagoner and a farmer, but he loved being a soldier. He knew that without an education he would have trouble starting a new career. Still, if he could not be treated fairly in the army, he would give it up. Many of his supporters asked him to stay. Morgan refused. He returned to Soldier's Rest.

Back at home he found that Abigail had worked the land while he was away. But their home and other buildings needed many repairs. He got busy on the repairs and returned to farming.

9.
Southern Campaign

From his farm Morgan kept up with the war through friends who wrote to him. Of all the news he received, the most alarming was that the British government had decided to move the fighting to the South.

Word came in early summer of 1776 that British ships were sailing toward Charles Town, South Carolina. A rumor spread the enemy planned to capture the city and make South Carolina an example to the other colonies.

Charlestonians hurried to defend their city. They tore down warehouses along the coast to make room for cannons. They started building a fort from palmetto trees on Sullivan's Island to defend the harbor.

Charles Town Harbor

Sooner than expected, British ships sailed in. Cannons thundered. To the Americans' delight, ammunition fired from the ships stuck in the tough, elastic-like palmetto logs of the fort or landed in the loose beach sand. The fort received no damage. Defeated, the British fleet pulled back out to sea.

Later the British gained control of Savannah, Georgia, and from there moved back into South Carolina. Along their way to Charles Town, the British plundered plantations, frightening women and children. They burned houses and churches and carried off slaves.

Charles Town already suffered from a smallpox epidemic and lack of food. When the British shells began to rain on the city, the Patriots had no choice but to surrender.

From the city port, the British set up forts over South Carolina where they continued their

cruelty toward American families. Their actions even caused some Tories who had been loyal to the British to switch sides and fight with the Patriots. The situation in the South did not look good.

10.
Morgan Returns

News reached Morgan of General Horatio Gates's terrible defeat in Camden, South Carolina. British Lord Cornwallis and the feared Banastre Tarleton threatened the South. It looked as though the Patriots were losing the war.

For twelve months Morgan had enjoyed his family and home. Now he put aside his personal feelings and set out to join General Nathanael Greene in Charlotte, North Carolina.

Greene had just replaced Gates as commander in chief of the southern forces.

Greene knew his small, mostly untrained force could not compete with the large British army. As an avid reader, Greene had studied many books about army strategy. Based on that knowledge, he decided to split his army to make it hard for the British to keep up with them.

Greene had heard of the rugged, hard-fighting Virginia rifleman named Daniel Morgan. He knew he could count on him and his sharpshooters. He wasted no time in handing over half of his army to Morgan.

Greene wrote to Colonel Morgan:

Sir:

You are appointed to the command of a corps of light infantry, a detachment of militia, and Lieutenant Colonel William Washington's regiment of light dragoons. Others may join you.

With these troops you will proceed to the west side of Catawba River. You are to give protection to that part of the country and spirit up the American people. You will try to prevent plundering and give receipts to friends of the independence of America if you take food or animals from them.

You and your militia will harry the British and keep me advised of your movements and those of your enemy through your scouts.

I entrust you with this command.

Given under my hand at Charlotte, this 16th December 1780.

Nath. Greene

11.
The Chase

Morgan accepted Greene's offer and set out through the southern states to build up his army. Men who knew of his reputation went with him. Colonel Andrew Pickens of South Carolina brought his men to join with Morgan's troop.

When Cornwallis heard Greene had divided his army, he had no choice but to divide his own. He sent the dreaded Colonel Banastre Tarleton and his Green Dragoons after Morgan. "Wipe him out!" Cornwallis ordered. "Catch him and smash him."

Cruel Tarleton was good at carrying out orders like that. "I will destroy him and his men," he said, "or push them into the Broad River."

Four days of winter marching in soaking rains took Morgan and his men sixty miles south of Charlotte, North Carolina. They set up camp at Grindal Shoals on the Pacolet River in South Carolina.

Tarleton learned of Morgan's location. Dressed in their bright green and scarlet uniforms and hailed by flags, the well-fed British troops set out after the Patriots.

Except for the Continentals and state troops under Morgan's command, none wore uniforms. Others wore hunting clothes. All were underfed and in need of clothing. Morgan worked extra hard to keep their spirits up.

All the while, each side had scouts spying on the other. Morgan's scouts reported that Tarleton's men struggled for two days trying to

get men, provisions, and artillery across the swollen waters of the Enoree and Tyger Rivers.

Not long after the last scout report, a boy came into camp leading a wagon pulled by a bull. The boy was returning home from selling potatoes to the British.

"My daddy told me to listen while I was there," he said, "and to come over here and tell what I heard." His voice raised in excitement, he told them Colonel Tarleton was coming after Morgan with a thousand men.

One of the Patriot scouts confirmed the boy's story. Tarleton was on his way. From the location given of the enemy camp, Morgan figured the Pacolet River would slow the British march. But they were, at the most, no more than five miles away.

Morgan's first thought was to stand and fight. But he knew he couldn't do that without a plan. If Tarleton overtook them on the road, they'd all be cut down by British bayonets.

Morgan was not far from the Broad River, but if he ordered his men to cross it to get away, many of his militia would desert him.

He saw no choice but to stand and fight. Still, he had to choose the right spot to survive the battle.

He had a sudden idea. Why hadn't he thought of it before? Everybody in the region was familiar with the cow pens, that high-rolling land near the North Carolina line. Farmers used it as pastureland to hold cattle before taking them to market.

With renewed energy, Morgan gave orders for his officers to move their men toward Thicketty Creek. "Our final destination is the cow pens," he told them. "Tonight our men will have a meal and a night's rest before the battle."

The chase would soon be over.

12.
The Plan

Early the next morning scouts rushed into Morgan's camp to announce that Tarleton had crossed the Pacolet River and was headed toward them.

Morgan shouted for the wagons to be loaded. The men preparing breakfast around small fires scrambled to their feet, grabbed their half-cooked cornmeal cakes and stuffed them in their mouths. Soon the Patriot army slogged along the slick, muddy Green River Road.

It was hard going, but Morgan pushed them on, bawling commands to the soldiers and the teamsters.

Since he had chosen to make the stand at Cowpens, Morgan and his top officers moved on ahead of the column of soldiers. He was eager to see the site with the battle in mind.

Morgan knew he couldn't ask for better officers. Colonel Eager Howard commanded the Maryland and Delaware Continentals. Tall, raw-boned Colonel Andrew Pickens, called Wizard Owl by the Cherokees, was nothing like Morgan. He never laughed and rarely smiled, but Morgan knew him as a loyal leader whose militia respected him. Colonel William Washington, commanding the saber-armed cavalry, would get into the fight when he was needed to protect the militia from the feared British bayonets.

As they rode into the meadow, Morgan liked what he saw. The land rose to form a ridge.

A thin growth of oak, hickory, and pine trees speckled the sloping ground. After a distance, the ground dipped and rose again to a higher ridge. Behind that second ridge was a shallow low ground, much like a drainage basin, called a swale.

To his surprise the swale was deep enough to protect men on horseback from enemy fire. Yet if the cavalry stood in their stirrups, they could look down across the wooded meadow. Morgan couldn't believe his luck.

In the fading light of the winter evening, he turned to his officers. "We can trap 'em," he said. "We can lead 'em on and when we've led 'em far enough, we'll hit 'em with everything we got."

Morgan could tell the officers did not feel the excitement he did. He hurried to convince them. "Look here," he said in his strong backwoods accent, "we'll put the men in three lines. In front we'll put 150 hand-picked sharpshooters. Hiding behind the scattered trees and tall grass, they can pick off the officers and then fall back to the second line.

"We'll put a second line of militia a hundred yards behind the sharpshooters. We'll instruct 'em to do the same as the first group— take aim, fire twice, and retreat to the rear behind Billy's cavalry. He'll be waiting there to finish the scoundrels off."

One of the officers blurted out that the militia would run from British artillery fire without firing a shot.

Knowing this was true, Morgan came back with, "Where they going to run? We'll have our backs to the Broad River. They'd never make it across the river along this section." Then he let out one of his bellowing laughs. "You just leave that idea about running to me. I'll take care of it."

And his officers knew that one way or another he would.

Assured of his officers' support for his plan, Morgan lowered his voice and said, "On this ground I will beat 'Banny' Tarleton or I will lay down my bones."

13.
Pep Rally

As night fell, Morgan herded his men into the swale. Soon campfires burned to prepare food from supply wagons. Horses tied safely on the far edge of the swale whinnied and rolled their eyes. Mounted scouts moved in and out among the soldiers. Noise and confusion filled the night.

Morgan's rheumatism and sciatica had bothered him since the beginning of the hard campaign in the Carolinas. On this frosty night he didn't let the pain stop him from doing his duty. Instead of retiring to his tent, he went from campfire to campfire encouraging the men and explaining exactly what he expected of them.

By the light of campfire and a Carolina moon, he passed among them. Morgan knew how to get the men fired up. He was a backwoodsman like many of them, and they trusted him.

"Don't give the British a chance at you," he told them. "They'll hack you with a bayonet and hang you."

Turning to his aide, he bellowed, "Here, Major, pull up my shirt and show 'em what the British did to my back."

Soldiers crowded around. By the light of the campfire they stared at the purple welts across his back.

"The British burned your houses, killed your cattle, and stole your chickens," he said. "They scared your womenfolks.

I wanta see you do something about it."

To the militia, Morgan said, "You been wanting to run. You gonna get your chance. All you gotta do is hold up your head and fire two shots. Then you can turn and run. You'll not be running away, but the British will think you are and come after you. That's when we'll get 'em. And don't worry about your comrades shooting you. They'll hold their fire until you run back through the line." He let out a hearty laugh and added, "That is, if you don't run too slow.

"Now you Carolina and Georgia boys are gonna be lined up right alongside each other. I been hearing your tall tales about who's the best. Now you got your chance to prove it, and the rest of us are gonna be up on that slope looking down at you."

Buoyed by Morgan's pep talk, men poked each other in the ribs and talked big.

"My boys," he said in a more serious tone, "victory will bring you glory. When you return home, old folks will cheer you and girls will kiss your cheeks."

Far into the night he walked among the men, cheering them up. "This old wagoner," he said of himself, "is going to crack his horse whip over 'Banny,' but he needs your help."

Morgan liked to joke with his men about Tarleton, but he knew Colonel Banastre Tarleton was no joke.

Long after the men rolled into their blankets, Morgan went over the plans with his officers. Afterwards he waited for Pickens's scouts to report Tarleton's position.

"I believe," wrote one of Morgan's officers in his report after the battle, "that Morgan didn't get a moment's sleep all that night."

14.
The Battle

In the cold gray dawn of the next day, Pickens's scouts galloped into camp with news that Tarleton was headed up Green River Road. Minutes later Morgan hurried through the tents shouting, "Boys, get up! Banny's coming!"

Soldiers struggled to their feet and bolted down cold hominy cooked the night before. Wagoners hitched their teams, piled provisions on the wagons, and jolted them off to a safe place at the rear of the battlefield. The cavalry ran for their horses.

Ignoring the pain in his hip, Morgan made sure the horses of militia assigned to front lines were tied to trees under guard and out of the line of fire. Then he rode down to the riflemen under Pickens who would give the command to open fire. He praised them for their courage in other skirmishes when they had no help from Continentals or the cavalry.

"Remember," he said, "just two shots. Right in the gizzard of the officers!"

By now the Patriot officers had arranged their units on the battlefield in three lines, according to Morgan's plan. One hundred fifty riflemen made up the first line. They hid in the grass and behind the scattered trees. The bulk of the militia made up the second line. The main line, in third position on the crest of the rising slope, was made up of Continentals and Virginia militia. Behind the slope the infantry waited in the swale, ready to emerge at any time to support the front lines.

In setting up his strategy, Morgan planned to do something dangerous. He would leave the flanks open. His plan was this: the front line would fire twice, then fall back to the second line. The combined line would fire, picking out the officers' uniforms as targets. As the British troops got close, the militia would circle around the left side of the third line, getting behind the Continentals.

As they waited for the British attack, Morgan rode along each line. In his raspy voice, he shouted orders. To the sharpshooters he croaked, "Hold your fire 'til they're a hundred paces from you!"

Morgan was proud of his men. They had a record of bravery on the battlefield. He understood that men followed leaders who

Patriots

WASHINGTON'S CAVALRY

Ridge

Ridge

HOWARD'S CONTINENTALS

PICKENS'S MILITIA

SHARPSHOOTERS

BANASTRE TARLETON

REDCOATS AND DRAGOONS

British

LARGE BRITISH ARMY

respected them. How many times had he told them "I will not ask you to go into danger where I don't join you"?

Waiting, the men stamped their feet and blew on their hands to keep warm. Finally, the sun rose over the slopes of Thicketty Mountain. A deathlike quiet fell over the field. All eyes peered toward the tree line where the British would break through.

Suddenly green-coated dragoons and red-coated infantry appeared. Then as quickly as they appeared, they stopped. An officer in a green coat rode out into the clearing. It was the dreaded Banastre Tarleton. Artillerymen wheeled out the cannon, a three-pounder. To each side of it, Redcoats formed a line. At the ends of the line, Tarleton posted fifty dragoons.

The British line advanced in a sort of trot, stopped, and called out "Halloo!"

From the crest of the slope Morgan bellowed, "They gave us a British 'halloo,' boys. Give 'em an Indian one!"

The Patriots howled in blood-curdling Indian war cries.

In answer Tarleton ordered the green jackets on horseback to attack.

Patriot skirmishers, who lay in the tall grass and crouched behind young pines, heard and felt the thud of hoofbeats pounding up the slope. They saw the flash of sunlight on the bayonets.

Pickens's order of "Fire!" rang out.

In puffs of smoke rising from the crackle of rifle fire, Patriots saw horses fall or rear up and turn back. Saddles emptied. Survivors retreated.

Upset and angry, Tarleton shouted, "Fire the cannon point-blank!"

Most of the three-pound cannonballs shot too high. Instead of causing harm, they whizzed over the heads of the militia  who fired their two shots and turned to run back to the second line.

Thinking the soldiers were retreating, the British line of scarlet and green jackets moved forward. Howard's militia met them head on. His seasoned veterans poured round after round into the advancing troops. The militia then dashed around the seasoned Continentals, positioning themselves behind the last line.

Again, Tarleton thought the Patriots were running from the fight. Loudly his drums rolled and the fifes shrilled. He ordered another charge.

Morgan raced over the slope, thundering after the few Patriots who tried to flee the battlefield. Another boom of his voice sent Washington's cavalry like a whirlwind into the saber fight to protect retreating militia.

For a time, the militia became confused and

started to withdraw. When Morgan saw what was happening, he rallied them. Brandishing his sword in the air, he shouted, "Form, form, my brave fellows! Follow me!"

The two forces faced each other on the slope, shrouded in smoke. Lines broke and the enemies went at each other hand to hand with bayonets and sabers.

Taken by surprise at the unexpected force of the Patriot army, British soldiers panicked and threw down their arms. Tarleton could not get his dragoons to reenter the fight. During the confusion, he escaped with some of his troops.

The battle lasted less than an hour.

Over 900 of Tarleton's 1100-man army were killed, wounded, captured, or missing. Morgan lost 72 men.

Although some Patriot soldiers shouted "Tarleton's Quarter," Morgan and his

officers ordered the men not be killed but taken prisoner.

After a hard-fought battle and attending to the wounded and dead on the battlefield, as well as the prisoners, Morgan praised his soldiers and officers. Then he retired to his tent to get a report off to Greene.

Little did he know the battle of Cowpens would become known as one of the greatest victories of the Southern Campaign or that it would make him a legendary hero.

By noon Morgan was on the road to meet General Greene.

15.
Honors

Morgan's sciatica had become too painful to remain in the saddle. He asked for a leave of absence to return home to Virginia.

In July 1781 he retired from the army, but he never forgot about his "boys" who had fought beside him. He wrote Congress that the soldiers needed clothes and food.

Morgan worked for his country in a different role from 1797 to 1799. He served in the House of Representatives.

Years later, he built another home. He named this stone house Saratoga for the battles he fought in New York.

After the battle of Cowpens, Congress

voted Daniel Morgan a gold medal. He did not, however, receive it until nine years later due to lack of money for casting.

In 1856, the Washington Light Infantry monument was erected on the Cowpens battlefield, which is now designated as a national historic site. The obelisk monument, first placed in the Morgan Hill area of the battlefield in 1932, stands today in front of the visitors center.

Since the Revolutionary War, Morgan's heroism has been honored in many ways. Among them is a bronze statue of him in downtown Spartanburg, South Carolina. Also, two military ships have honored the South Carolina battle with the name *USS Cowpens*, the first used in World War II.

Morgan died July 6, 1802. He was buried in the Winchester Presbyterian Church in Virginia. Later his body was moved to Mount Hebron Cemetery, also in Winchester. The Winchester-Frederick County Historical Society erected a granite monument of his likeness over his grave.

Although he had a fiery temper, Morgan's hearty laugh, good humor, and natural wit made him a favorite among his soldiers and his neighbors. His behavior was often rough, but he could be kind and tender. Above all, in the true nature of a hero, he was loyal to his friends and to the cause of freedom.

When General Greene heard of Morgan's death, he said, "Great generals are scarce. There are few Morgans to be found."

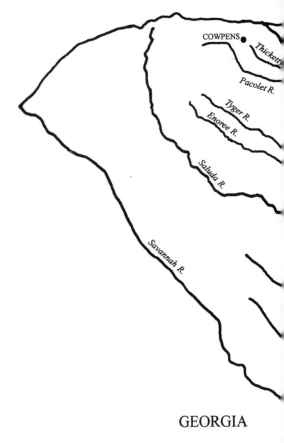

COWPENS

Thicketty

Pacolet R.

Tyger R.

Enoree R.

Saluda R.

Savannah R.

GEORGIA

South
Carolina

WORDS FOR UNDERSTANDING

ambush   a surprise attack by persons hiding; a hidden position

avid   eager

artillerymen persons who belong to an artillery unit; persons who use large guns and cannons

bawling   shouting

bellowing   a prolonged shouting in a deep voice

bog   wet, spongy ground

brandishing   waving

brawl   fight

buoyed   lifted [spirits]; cheered up

campaign   a series of planned military operations

cavalry   combat troops mounted on horses

commissioned   appointed

confirmed   proven to be true

convince   make someone agree

Continental   a paid soldier of the American colonies during the Revolutionary War

crest   the highest point

dragoons   heavily-armed soldiers who fought on horseback

epidemic   a disease spreading rapidly

fife   a small musical instrument like a flute

flank   the side of anything

forbade   did not allow

frontier   the border between settled and un-settled country

gizzard   in this case, stomach

harry	to worry or aggravate
infantry	combat soldiers on foot
jolted	shook up
legendary	describing ones whose deeds are handed down to following generations
militia	a volunteer group of soldiers, usually made up of ordinary citizens
panicked	became suddenly fearful
plundering	destroying property and taking goods by force
point-blank	straight ahead; aimed at a mark
provisions	food and other supplies gathered
rallied	encouraged back into action
rangers	troops on horseback who patrol an area
raspy	harsh; grating

receipts   written acknowledgements of receiving goods, to be paid for or replaced at a later time

reputation   the way a person's character is seen by others

reverence   a feeling of respect

rheumatism   painful condition of joints and muscles

rowdy   displaying rough behavior

rumored   talked about as being real, but not necessarily true

saber   curved cavalry sword

sacrificing   giving up, as Morgan giving up his health

sciatica   a painful condition of the hip and thigh involving the sciatic nerve

scoundrel   a rascal; a dishonest, no-good person

shrowded   covered

skirmishes	fights between small groups of troops
slogged	made one's way with great effort; worked hard at something
strategy	a plan of action for a large scale military operation
swale	a low area of land
tactics	plans of action in war
tavern	a building where alcohol is sold to be drunk there; also, an inn, where travelers sleep and get meals
treason	betrayal of one's country
wagoner	a person who drives a supply wagon
warehouses	buildings where goods are stored
welts	raised ridges on the skin left by a slash or blow

THINGS TO DO AND THINK ABOUT

1. There were many meadows in upstate South Carolina like the one where the battle of Cowpens was fought. In January 1781, this one was known locally as the cow pens. The name came about from the custom of upcountry stock raisers wintering their cattle in the green valley around Thicketty Mountain. The spot became famous after Daniel Morgan chose it for his battle site. Of course there is now a town named Cowpens. Do you know where your town or city got its name?

    You might be interested in making a model of the strategy Morgan worked out to defeat the British. You could also photocopy page 54 and draw lines to show how the soldiers followed through with the plan. Morgan's plan was different from that used by commanding officers at this time in history: standing soldiers in one, long, straight line to face the enemy. Explain to a friend how placement of the soldiers at Cowpens won the battle.

2. Do you think if Daniel had lived in today's world he might have tried to contact his parents later in his life? What would have made the difference?

3. Write a character sketch of Daniel Morgan. Brainstorm first by making a list, answering the following

questions: What was he like? What were his character traits? Does one trait stand out above the others? How did he look? How did he talk? How did he feel about other people? Did other people like being with him? Do you think he changed as he got older? If so, in what ways? (Get your ideas organized by numbering what you will tell first, and so on. You do not have to use everything you have written down.) Once you have completed your planning, open your character sketch with a sentence that might introduce Morgan to a reader who has never heard of him. Close your sketch by showing why we honor him today.

4. Morgan said he had come to realize that a man's worth is measured by the way he acts and talks now, not on what he has done in the past. Explain the meaning of this and cite someone you know personally to prove this is true.

5. Morgan told soldiers he recruited for the army that he had "an old score to settle with the British." What did he mean?

6. Do you see any comparison between what Morgan did with his men the night before the Cowpens battle to what today's athletic coaches do? Explain.

7. Music from drums and fifes made soldiers' lives more bearable during the marches, in camp, and in battle. Drums were also used to communicate during battle as drum beats reached soldiers better than most officers' voices. Although we have no account of a very young drummer at the battle of Cowpens, it is said that after the battle Morgan picked up his nine-year-old drummer and kissed him on both cheeks. How do you think you would feel as a drummer in such a battle? Would you like to research how drums and fifes are used in battle? Did you know they can command soldiers to do many things, even "strike tents," meaning to take them down?

8. Do you know why some cannons are called "grass-hoppers"? It is because they could be supported by a pair of legs instead of wheels. They also jumped when fired. Grasshoppers were pulled along on wheeled carriages and could travel at great speed.

9. The medal Morgan received from Congress read "Victory Vindicates Liberty." What do you think that means?

10. Morgan fought with Benedict Arnold at the battle of Quebec. For many generations Arnold's name has been linked with treason. Would you like to find out

what his connection is with West Point? By the way, did you know Arnold was a pharmacist by trade?

11. In 1845 a painter, William Ranney, recreated the scene of the Cowpens battle in oil. He read about the battle in George Washington's biography written by John Marshall. From that account and stories he had heard, he imagined how it would have looked. You can see this painting by looking up the Battle of Cowpens on the Internet.

12. Did you know that two military ships have been named *Cowpens*? You can learn more about them at the Cowpens National Battlefield visitors center in Cowpens, South Carolina. There is also a "Mighty Moo" Festival held in the town of Cowpens each year. Incidentally, the name "Mighty Moo" has nothing to do with cows. It comes from the churning sound made by the original *USS Cowpens*, a World War II aircraft carrier.

13. It is hard to keep up with the different kinds of Patriot soldiers who fought in the Revolutionary War. In Morgan's army there were Continentals, militia, and cavalry. All three fought in the battle at Cowpens.

    The **Continentals** were considered the standing army. Each state was required to recruit, uniform, and supply regiments for the Continental Army. These soldiers enlisted for three years and were considered to be better trained than others. A Continental Infantry, meaning soldiers on foot, formed in Delaware, Maryland, Virginia, and the Carolinas. They fought under Lieutenant Colonel John Eager Howard. Their weapons were muskets with bayonets.

The **militia** were citizen soldiers called from their homes when danger threatened. Most were soldiers for short periods of time. Some states drafted men to serve. Chiefly, Morgan's militia came from the western part of the Carolinas. Since Georgia was occupied by the British at this time, Georgians fought with South Carolina companies. Some Virginians who volunteered in Morgan's militia had served in the Continental Army. These soldiers now served under General Andrew Pickens. Most carried rifles. A few had muskets.

The **cavalry** fought on horseback. The Continental Light Dragoons, called state troops, from the Carolinas and Virginia, fought under Lieutenant Colonel William Washington. Dragoons served on horseback or foot, always ready for either duty. They generally fought with sword in hand after the first shot was fired.

14. Did you know that Lieutenant Colonel William Washington was a distant cousin of George Washington? The story is told that Colonel Washington, called

"Billy" by Morgan, once made a fake cannon. He and his men patrolled an area between Charlotte, North Carolina, and Camden, South Carolina, when he heard Tories had made a fort of a barn in nearby Rugely's Mill.

Washington knew he could do nothing with the small guns they carried. Then he had an idea about a trick that might drive the Tories out. He took a pine log and propped it up to make it look like a cannon. He called out to the Tories to surrender or he would blow them to bits. The Tory colonel took a look at the Patriots' artillery and immediately surrendered.

After the war William Washington married a South Carolina girl, and they settled in Charleston. Their home still stands on South Battery. Before their marriage, Jane Elliot made a red silk flag from her draperies for Washington's troop. It was carried in the battle of Cowpens. Today the flag is in the care of the Light Infantry Corps of Charleston.

15. If possible, visit the Cowpens National Battlefield that preserves the scene of the battle in upstate South Carolina. It is eleven miles northwest of Gaffney by way of S.C. 11. For further information or reservations, call (864) 461-2828, write Cowpens National Battlefield, Post Office Box 308, Chesnee, S.C. 29323, or contact the park online at www.nps.gov/cowp.

SOURCES USED

Agniel, Lucien. "Rout at Cowpens." *Sandlapper Magazine*, June 1971, 89-90.

Babits, Lawrence E. *Cowpens Battlefield: A Walking Guide.* Johnson City, TN: The Overmountain Press, 1993.

———. *Devil of a Whipping*: *The Battle of Cowpens.* Chapel Hill, NC: University of North Carolina Press, 1998.

Edgar, Walter. *South Carolina: A History.* Columbia, SC: University of South Carolina Press, 1970.

Fleming, Thomas J. "Downright Fighting." *Official National Park Handbook.* National Park Service, 1988.

Higginbotham, Don. *Daniel Morgan: Revolutionary Rifleman.* Chapel Hill: University of North Carolina Press, 1961.

Hilborn Nat, and Sam Hilborn. *Battleground of Freedom.* Columbia, SC: Sandlapper Press, 1970.

Pancake, John S. *This Destructive War: The British Campaign in the Carolinas,* 1780-1782. Tuscaloosa, AL: University of Alabama Press, 1985.

Ripley, Warren. *Battleground: South Carolina in the Revolution.* Charleston, SC: *Evening Post* Publishing Company, 1983.

Roberts, Kenneth. *The Battle of Cowpens: The Great Morale Builder.* Mattituck, NY: American Reprint Company, 1976.

Weekes, Bill. "A Legacy Bovine and Mighty." *Sandlapper Magazine,* Summer 2001, 62-63.

Internet Sites:
  www.patriotresource.com/battles/cowpens.html
  www.nps.gov/cowp/dmorgan.htm

ABOUT THE AUTHOR

Idella Bodie was born in Ridge Spring, South Carolina. She received her degree in English from Columbia College and taught high school English and creative writing for thirty-one years.

Ms. Bodie's first book was published in 1971, and she has been writing books for young readers ever since. This is her nineteenth book.

Ms. Bodie lives in Aiken with her husband Jim. In her spare time, she enjoys reading, gardening, and traveling.

OTHER BOOKS BY IDELLA BODIE:

Carolina Girl: A Writer's Beginning
Ghost in the Capitol
Ghost Tales for Retelling
A Hunt for Life's Extras: The Story of Archibald Rutledge
The Mystery of Edisto Island
The Mystery of the Pirate's Treasure
The Secret of Telfair Inn
South Carolina Women
Stranded!
Trouble at Star Fort
Whopper

"Heroes and Heroines of the American Revolution" Series
The Man Who Loved the Flag
The Secret Message
The Revolutionary Swamp Fox
The Fighting Gamecock
Spunky Revolutionary War Heroine
The Courageous Patriot
Quaker Commander
Brave Black Patriots